SURTSEY

THE NEWEST PLACE ON EARTH

SURTSEY
THE NEWEST PLACE ON EARTH

KATHRYN LASKY

▲

PHOTOGRAPHS BY CHRISTOPHER G. KNIGHT

Hyperion Books for Children
New York

Acknowledgment

We would like to thank Einar Gustavsson, the Icelandic Tourist Bureau, and Jeanne Hanson for their invaluable help in getting us to Surtsey. We would also like to thank the Surtsey Society for granting us permission to stay on the island.

–K. L., C. K.

Text copyright © 1992 by Kathryn Lasky. Photographs copyright © 1992 by Christopher G. Knight.
All rights reserved.
Printed in the United States of America. For more information address
Hyperion Books for Children, 114 Fifth Avenue, New York, NY 10011
First Edition
1 3 5 7 9 10 8 6 4 2

Library of Congress Cataloging-in-Publication Data

Lasky, Kathryn.
Surtsey: the newest place on Earth / Kathryn Lasky: photos by
Christopher Knight — 1st ed.
p. cm.
Summary: Describes formation, naming, and colonization of the
twenty-seven-year-old volcanic island Surtsey and how
the first animals and plants became established there.
ISBN 1-56282-300-0 (trade) — ISBN 1-56282-301-9 (lib. bdg.)
1. Surtsey (Iceland) — Juvenile literature. 2. Island ecology — Iceland —
Surtsey — Juvenile literature. [1. Surtsey (Iceland) 2. Island ecology —
Iceland — Surtsey. 3. Ecology — Iceland — Surtsey.]
I. Knight, Christopher G., ill. II. Title.
GB478.58.L37 1992 508.4912 — dc20 92-52990 CIP AC

All photographs by Christopher G. Knight, except: Sigurdur Thorarisson: pp. 2, 4, 11, 12, 23, 27, 30,
32, 34, 48, and 50 (top). Sigurgeir Jónasson: pp. 7, 15, 19, 20, 24, 28, 29, 31, 40, and 64.

The text for this book is set in 14-point ITC Novarese Book.

Contents

Attribution

The quotations that open each chapter are adapted from an Icelandic epic, *The Prose Edda*, written down by Snorri Sturluson in the years 1220 to 1230. The *Edda* contained poetry of the Vikings as well as many Scandinavian myths and ancient stories of the Norse gods. Snorri Sturluson, a historian, poet, and politician, was Christian, but he had a deep understanding of why the sagas and myths had a profound meaning for humans living in harsh and unpredictable environments. The first part of the *Edda*, the "Gylfagninning," or "The Deluding of Gylfi," tells the story of the creation and the end of the world as well as the adventures of Norse gods. Gylfi was a legendary king of Sweden, but he also appears as a sea king in Norse mythology.

1 THE NEWEST PLACE ON EARTH

It was at the beginning of time, when nothing was; sand was not, nor sea, nor cool waves. Earth did not exist, nor heaven on high. The mighty gap was, but there was no growth....

This is the place where people go to measure the flowers. This is the place where the animals have come one kind at a time—a bird, a seal, a fly. And often they have come alone, without a mate, at intervals over the years. This is the place where once upon a time was just twenty-nine years ago. This is the newest place on earth. This is Surtsey island.

Surtsey came into being a few hours before dawn on Tuesday, November 14, 1963. It was not a gentle birth. It erupted squalling and full of fire from the Atlantic Ocean near Vestmannaeyjar, or the Westman Islands, south of Iceland.

Its beginnings were witnessed by the crew of the *Isleifur* II, an Icelandic fishing vessel casting four miles to the south of the site of the eruption.

The story of the newest place on earth is one of the oldest. It was told in the Norse myths that had described extraordinary events of nature. Now the story told long ago was coming true again. And for the fishermen of the *Isleifur*, once upon a time was now.

Surtsey Island with a view of the two major craters ▶

2 THE ERUPTION—A SAGA COMES TO LIFE

Surtur travels from the south with fire....
The sun will go dark, earth will sink into the sea.
From heaven will vanish bright stars. Steam surges and...
high flames flicker against the very sky.

Afterward some people would say that they had smelled the strange sulfurous odor for a week or more preceding the eruption. In Reykjavík, 70 miles away, sensing devices that monitor for earthquakes reported a slight tremor in the region weeks before the actual eruption—a condition that is not exceptional in Iceland, a country noted for its frequent volcanic eruptions. In the ocean near the site, there had merely been a slight rise in the water's temperature.

All was quiet on the day of the eruption. The tiny arctic terns zipped down from the sky, skimming the ocean's surface in search of food. Puffins made shallow dives for minnows, and elegant gannets and cormorants plunged from high above for endless meals of fish. The surface was still, but deep under the sea an old story was beginning.

The crew of the *Isleifur* had begun to smell the strong sulfurous odor at 6:55 that Tuesday morning. Next, the boat seemed rocked by a strange movement, as if caught in a whirlpool. Then, in the half light of the dawn, the crew noticed something dark and smoking rising out of the sea. The time was 7:15 A.M. Was there a ship on fire? They radioed the coast guard, but no fires had been reported.

▲ *The first days of the eruption, November 17 through November 19, 1963*

Indeed there was a fire—one that had been burning almost 400 feet below the surface of the sea for perhaps many days. On this Tuesday, the fire had reached the surface. Water began to sizzle, and from a distance what seemed like an immense bouquet of black feathers spurted toward the sky. The feathers were topped by a huge cauliflower cloud. The dark feathery bouquet and its cauliflower crown were full of steam, cinder, ash, rock, and pumice—lightweight volcanic glass that is puffed up by gas. (All of these airborne products of a volcano are called *tephra*.) By eight o'clock in the morning the crew estimated that there were two or three of these feathery columns of tephra, each reaching 200 feet high. And just two hours later the columns reached a height of 11,500 feet—or two miles into the sky!

It was risky for the Isleifur to sail near the eruption of the submarine volcano. Lava bombs the size of small cars were being hurled a thousand feet into the air, and they could easily land on a fishing vessel and ignite it. Through the thick veils of smoke, steam, and cinders, the pilot could barely see to steer the ship. Even breathing could be difficult as the fire from under the sea gulped all the available oxygen.

But a submarine eruption—even in Iceland—is something special. Perhaps there was a chance that an island might emerge, a new place on earth be created. Perhaps the column of fire and steam and rock might become this new place. The captain brought his ship close enough to study the eruption for a brief, tense period of time.

By three o'clock on Tuesday afternoon the crew of the Isleifur were not the only witnesses. The column of cinder and ash and steam stretched four miles high and could be see in Reykjavík.

As they watched, a northerly wind began to blow, stretching the dark tephra column and the lighter columns of cloud vapors into cocks' tails from which thinner veils of ash rained down over the sea and onto the deck of the Isleifur. The sun turned black and the sea glowed with embers. Flashes of lightning streaked up through the tephra columns to rake the sky. The materials from the eruption were electrified, and when they collided with the positively charged vapor clouds, there was a sky-shattering flash of light as the immense electrical burden was discharged.

That evening, at the base of the erupting plume of dark feathers, just under the surface of the water, there rose something darker than the night sea, and it did not move. It was solid. The ocean was breaking against it. The top of the cinder cone broke free from the sea. Like a black crown it rose from the water. A volcano.

By Wednesday morning—just twenty-four hours after the first eruption—an island was born.

From the vents of the volcano's cone, tails of ash, dust, and cinders continued to sweep across the sky. The ocean began to glow with embers as Surtsey broke from the sea. The eruption would continue at intervals for nearly four years.

◀ *The tephra column reaches nearly four miles high, November 16, 1963*

3 THE MID-ATLANTIC RIDGE

Loki had three children. One was Ferris the wolf, the second was the Midgard serpent, the third was Hel....These three siblings were brought up in Giantland. From them great mischief and disaster would arise....Then the ocean will surge up on to the lands because the Midgard serpent will fly into a giant rage and make its way ashore....

No creature from literature has been called more rotten names than the Midgard Serpent. Ugly Ring, Water-soaked Earth Band, Deadly-cold Serpent, and Twisted Bay-Menacer are but a few of the insulting names given it by the Norse saga writers. Earth scientists simply call it the Mid-Atlantic Ridge. It is a geologic reality, not a fictional creature.

The Mid-Atlantic Ridge is a submarine ridge that belts the earth along the middle of the ocean floor from the Arctic to the Antarctic. In only one place on its route, however, does the ridge heave itself out of the ocean. That place is Iceland, and its location explains why Iceland has so many volcanic eruptions. The country is situated smack in the middle of the serpent's course. And wherever the serpent twitches, the earth convulses—the ocean explodes and fire is spit into the sky.

As magma reaches the surface, a lava fountain shoots skyward. ▶

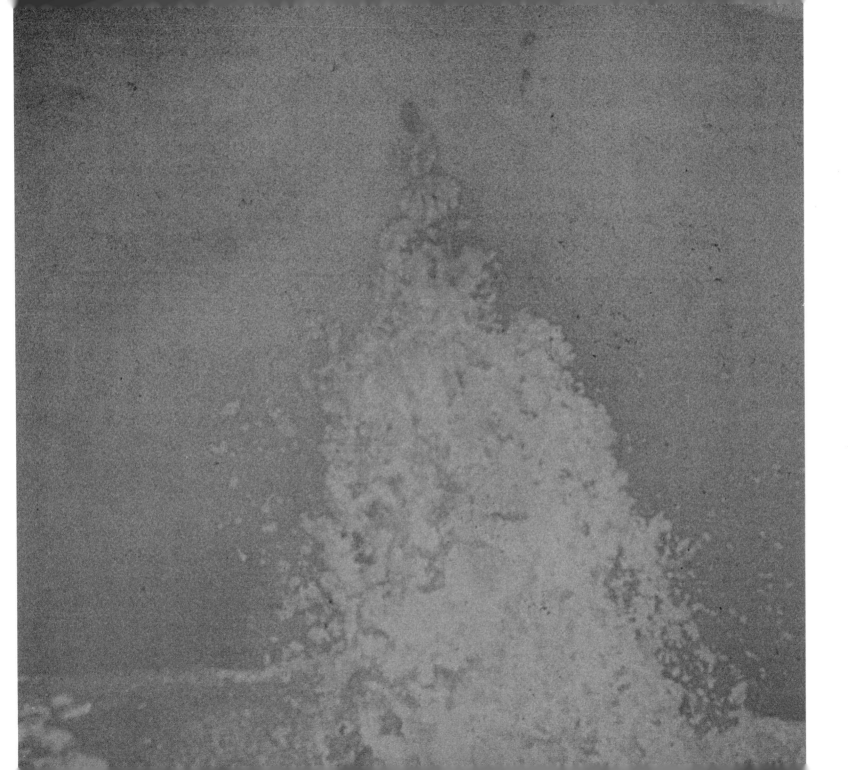

This is why: The earth is a sphere made up of layers. The top layer is the crust, where life occurs. Humans, animals, plants live here. Not all of the crust is visible, however; some of it is covered with oceans and soil. The crust, scientists have learned, is not just one whole chunk. Similar to a jigsaw puzzle, it is made up of pieces called plates. The layer beneath the crust is the mantle. The mantle is made up of hot rock, and nothing can live there.

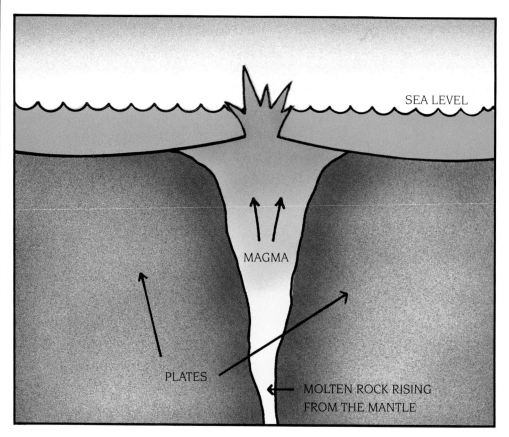

▲ *Mid-Atlantic ridge showing volcanic activity at the point where the plates tear apart.*

Hot rock is also called *molten rock*, or *magma*, and it can flow like hot tar. Although it is hard to imagine, the crust where we live actually floats on this deep, deep sea of molten hot rock. The plates of the crust then sail about like little ships on a sea of tar. They do not sail quickly—just a few inches every year—and their cargo is whatever is on top of them—oceans, islands, or even entire continents.

In places called *rifts* the plates tear apart from each other. Then molten rock in the mantle sometimes squishes out of the rift. Over hundreds of thousands of years, molten rock, welling up from the rifts under the sea, has hardened into a series of ridges. These ridges run like a belt, a seam, or, some might say, a serpent across the floor of the earth's ocean all around the globe. In the Mid-Atlantic Ridge the plates move apart. In the mid-ocean ridge of the Pacific the plates collide, with one sliding under another. Whether the plates pull apart or collide, the result is the same—

magma from the earth's mantle wells up, causing volcanic eruptions and adding mass to the trailing edges of the plates.

Such volcanic activity—both beneath the surface of the sea and on dry land—has been recorded from the time the Viking sailors plied the icy waters in their slender dragon ships, more than a thousand years ago. In the 10,000 to 15,000 years since the last ice age, more than 150 volcanoes have been active in Iceland. Lava covers nearly one-tenth of the country's surface. As far back as the sixth century, Irish monks who found their way to Iceland in leather boats described flames leaping from the sea, which could only be the fires of submarine volcanic eruptions.

In Iceland everyone—including scientists—knows the sagas, the stories of their ancestors. These tales of the violence and the turmoil of the Norsemen's world, their warlike gods, their giant beasts that spit fire, seem to fit the geologic turmoil of the land. Although scientists know it is a ridge, they often call it a serpent, and they are alert to every wiggle: they know that when the serpent twitches extraordinary events can happen.

4 FORMATION OF THE ISLAND

The Midgard serpent will spit so much poison that it will bespatter all the sky and sea, and it will be very terrible....Amid this turmoil the sky will open and from it will ride Muspell from the world of fire. Surtur will ride in front, and both before and behind him there will be burning fire.

The hump along the serpent's back that rose out of the sea and became Surtsey on the morning of November 14 was actually part of the cinder cone that had been building from the sea floor almost 400 feet below. Its shape and contours shifted constantly. On the first day the rim of the cone was barely visible, but by the third day it had climbed more than 130 feet above the surface and looked like a ridge. On November 20, six days after the eruption, it had reached a height of 230 feet and looked like a mountain on the horizon.

In reality, the mountain was more of a long crest, split lengthwise down the center. Within the split, or *fissure*, was hot magma. When magma reaches the surface it is called *lava*. The fissure was open to the sea and the sea fought a hard battle against this new upstart, staging the ultimate geologic battle with air and water pitted against fire and earth.

In the myths that described these natural events Aegir was the god of the ocean and Iord was the goddess of the earth. Ymir, a giant, was seawater. Kolga was the waves and Hraesvelg, or Vind, was a giant in the form of an eagle from whose wings the wind came and stirred Kolga until she broke and frothed white foam. The god of fire was called Surtur.

An explosive rain of cinder and ash ▶

All of these natural elements—wind, water, fire, and rock—were locked in battle against one another as soon as the first rim of the cone emerged. For days the eruption would spew forth more materials, enlarging the cinder cone. Then the ocean, whipped by the wind, would rush into the fissure and break down the cinder hills and ridges that had begun to build. Each time the seawater came in contact with the magma deep in the vent there would be an explosion and a plume of tephra would spurt into the sky. Some of these explosions were forceful enough to power a city ten times the size of New York. Rock and ash flew upward at rates of 330 feet per second!

As long as the seawater had direct access to this big crack and the vents within it, the island's future was risky. Indeed, no one even dared call it an island yet. It was a lump of rock that could be washed away, blown off the face of the earth within hours or less. But nine days after the first eruption there was a tremendous explosion at one end of the fissure. The force of the blast blew up a 130-foot-high mountain and closed off the vent from the sea. The wind then whipped up from many different directions over the next few days, redistributing rocks, ashes, cinders, and pumice into huge piles and thick walls. A blockade against the sea was beginning to form.

Iord, goddess of the earth, was gaining. Ymir, Aegir, and Kolga were being beaten into a retreat. The sea could not penetrate that tephra wall. Lava could now begin to flow. It looked as if the island might stay and grow in size.

◀ *The island builds through continuing eruptions.*

5 TO NAME AN ISLAND

They took molten particles and sparks that were flying uncontrolled and had shot out of the world of Muspell and set them in the middle of the firmament of the sky both above and below to illuminate heaven and earth.

By this time many people had heard about the volcanic eruption off the Westman Islands. The tiny island struggling for a foothold in the tumultuous sea had riveted the attention of scientists and journalists around the world. A few Icelandic scientists had flown over the eruption site in planes to study it, and others had skirted the boiling waters around the island in boats. As soon as it became evident that the island might indeed become a permanent place on the ocean's charts, the scientists of Iceland decided it must have a name.

In Iceland, names and words are very important. The Icelandic language, which is actually a form of Norwegian spoken long ago, is one of the oldest languages in the world. The Icelandic people are very proud of their language. They treat it like a beautiful antique, polishing it continually by using the old words and expressions with precision and savoring every sound. No word is used casually, and everything from mountains to rivers to new technology must have a special name. These names are decided upon by a committee.

It is called the Place Names Committee, and its members convened early in December 1963 to think about a name for the new island. They decided to call the island Surtsey, in honor of Surtur, who had come with fire to fight the serpent, according to the creation myth of the *Edda*. The vent from which the gases and tephra escaped was named Surtur. In a sense the name givers were hedging their bets by coming up with two names—one for the island and one for the vent. For if indeed the island was eventually swallowed by the sea, the name Surtur could at least be used for the underwater part—the submarine volcano.

There were people, however, in the

▲ *Three months after Surtsey first emerged, a second crater erupts on February 2, 1964.*

Westman Islands who objected to a name given by mainlanders not islanders. It was an island after all. Let the mainlanders of Iceland name their own volcanoes. On December 13 some intrepid Westman islanders set out to rename the island in person. They had barely stepped ashore, calling the island Vesturey, or West Island, when Surtsey exploded in seeming anger, flinging mud and pumice at the visitors. The visitors escaped, without injury, and took their name with them.

Surtsey remained Surtsey.

Very soon, when it looked as if Surtsey was going to stay, scientists realized that this island might offer a unique opportunity

for them to gather a glimmering of what the earth had been like 4.5 billion years ago, when it first formed. Surtsey, they believed, could become a laboratory for observing how life first begins or colonizes—a kind of terrestrial telescope through which scientists could look back in time to see what might have occurred at the very beginning of life on earth. Surtsey is an exceptionally rare and special place. If the island could be used this way, it would need someone to protect it, to keep away over-anxious journalists or tourists or casual visitors. This island needed a baby-sitter and someone to monitor the scientific experiments that geologists were planning to set up.

That baby-sitter was Arne Jonsson. A hut was built for him in what was thought to be the safest spot on the island, but it was hardly safe and never quiet. "Sometimes," he said, "I woke up in the night falling from my bed with the earthquakes.... The island was moving all the time, like a heart." But Jonsson grew used to watching over this rambunctious baby island and only became nervous when Surtsey was quiet for too long. That was when the real mischief could begin.

◄ *Scientists observe Surtsey while the ground is still hot and the ocean seethes.*

6 THE FORMATION OF LAVA

The sun will go dark, earth sink in the sea. From heaven vanish bright stars. Steam surges and...
high flame flickers against the very sky.

By January 1964 a barrier had arisen to protect the magma in the vent of the crater from the water, and the activity in Surtur had slowed considerably. By February that crater ceased to erupt. But then north of Surtur a new crater erupted. The scientists called it Surtur 2. The tephra it flung into the air was very helpful in building walls against the sea. Then it, too, simmered down and became less explosive. By April a lava shield had formed within the shaft of the volcano, making the vent watertight. The magma was safe from the cold waters of the sea. Lava fountains started to bubble and eventually spouted thick ribbons of glowing red magma nearly 160 feet into the air, splashing down into the red-hot lava lake that was welling up in the crater. The surface of the lava was 65 feet above sea level.

Lava escaped from the crater lake in a variety of ways. Often the magma would spill over the rim of the crater and course down the slopes of the island in fiery red rivers. Sometimes it would cascade over the edge in thick, slow-moving waves; other times in thin sheets that gushed into the sea at more than 40 miles per hour. Lava was once measured as moving 1,000 feet every 15 seconds.

A fountain of embers spurts from a lava lake. ▶

The lava had as many movements as a dancer—it swept and streamed, it gushed and oozed, it flowed and flooded, and sometimes it went underground to be squeezed through tubelike tunnels that glowed red with their hot load and bulged on the surface of the island like a bodybuilder's veins. These tubes were formed by rivulets of lava. The surface of the rivulets cooled very quickly, hardened, and formed an outer shell, but inside, the insulated lava continued to flow. The leading edges of such lava flows are called *paws* or *snouts*. Oftentimes these paws looked more like giant lobster claws pinching the island in a red-hot grip.

Streams of rapidly cooling lava ran along the shoreline in tongues. The tongues often fractured into smaller glassy pieces that were then sucked out to sea. Lava material was constantly being bashed and smashed, pulverized and crushed by breakers, and then swept out by tides only to be carried in again, in smaller, finer pebbles and pieces. Within two or three years a beach of black sand formed.

Lava added not only beaches but also layers of new thickness, thus extending the surface area of the island.

▲ October 1966, *the action continues*

Within five months of the initial eruption Surtsey measured more than one-half square mile, one-third of which was covered in lava. The rest of the island was composed of tephra and the huge magma bombs that exploded when the molten rock hit the water. Four months later, in August 1964, the island had an area of almost three-quarters of a mile, more than one-third of which was covered with lava.

◀ *April 13, 1964: a lava river flows toward the sea.*

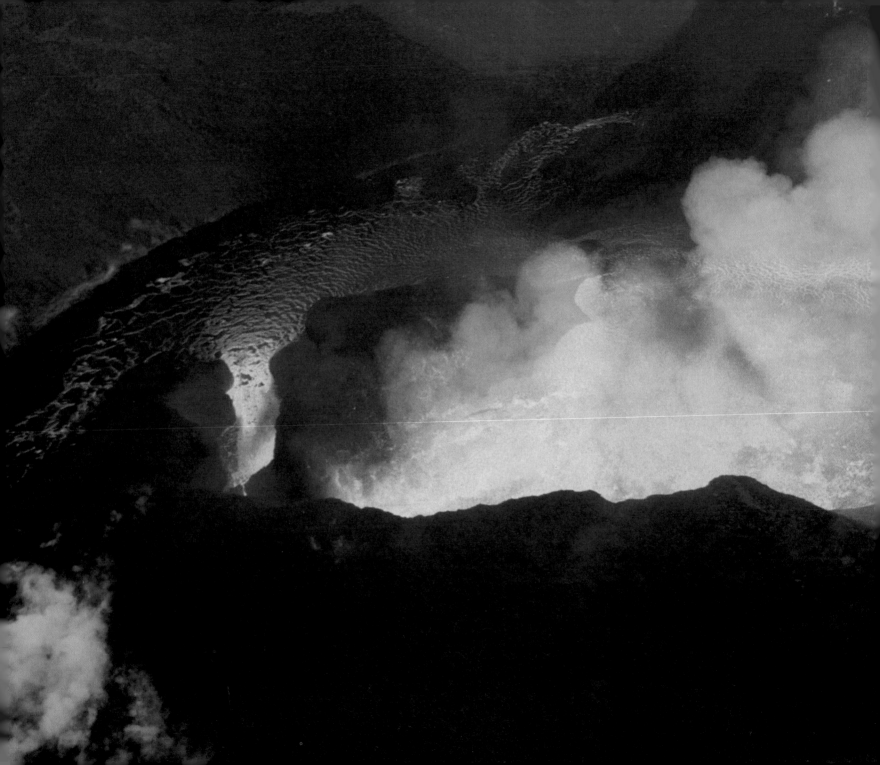

There are different names for lava, depending on its texture once it has solidified. *Hellu lava* is smooth-surfaced lava that has gushed and raced and twisted itself into shimmering smooth ropes. But when melted rock has moved slowly it results in a much rougher surface and is called *apal lava*.

The surface of Surtsey is often likened to a cake iced with black frosting, smooth with silky ropes in some places, studded with huge dark chocolate chips in others. And there are even some fields on Surtsey that look as if they are strewn with giant chunks of licorice.

When the tongues of lava reaching temperatures of 1100°C (2012°F) hit the cold water, a fringe of steam would swirl up. From an airplane it looked as if Surtsey wore a necklace of diamonds. And sometimes on clear nights Surtsey's glowing rivers of red lava could be seen coursing across her surface from more than one hundred miles away.

▲ *Flowing lava starts to cool.*

◄ *Between April 20 and April 23, 1964, a major lava flow begins.*

7 SCULPTING THE ISLAND—NEW FEATURES ARE ADDED

From Ymir's flesh was earth created, and from blood, the sea;
rocks of bones, trees of hair, and from his skull the sky.

It was through the lava that the island was shaped and sculpted, that cliffs were formed and black beaches like magicians' capes swept out into the sea.

The most recognizable shapes forged by the hot molten rock of any volcanoes are the lava domes, which are formed as lava oozes over the crater rims. The lava domes on Surtsey were changelings, though. They would rise up and then be destroyed by another eruption or worn away by wind.

The two major vents, Surtur 1 and Surtur 2, from which all the tephra, fire, and lava had erupted had become cone shaped as their outside slopes had built higher and higher around the craters within. These craters, called *nested craters*, surrounded by their rising cones, were now located on the middle and western sections of the island, which measured 2.8 square miles in total by the end of the eruption. Between Surtur 1 and Surtur 2 lay ridges and hills of cinders and ash.

◀ *Quiet but still changing after the last eruption*

▲ *An aerial view of the two craters, Surtur 1 and Surtur 2*

When tephra consolidates it begins to become something else. The Icelandic word is *moberg*. It is beige-colored rock, and it is very dense and very hard. Its geologic name is *palagonite*. It takes a few years for the tephra cones to become moberg. The two highest peaks on Surtsey are this type of formation. They reach 558 and 230 feet at their tops. On the north and west sides of Surtsey they take a very steep slant toward the sea and spill onto a level beach. It is not a straight smooth slant, however. The pale brown rock twists and runs into gullies, becoming great avenues for leading silt and mudflow materials to the beach and shoreline below.

A *moberg slope punctuated by a lava vent* ▶

The shoreline, a collar of lava surrounding the island, was continually battered by the sea. It retreated more; then, toward the end of April, the lava ceased flowing from the crater of Surtur 2. For a few days—less than a week—Kolga, goddess of the waves; Hraesvelg, the giant eagle of the wind; and Ymir, giant of the water, marshaled their forces and delivered a series of walloping gales. Wind, waves, and water scraped away at the cliffs relentlessly, until the high sheer lava walls dropped like black curtains into the sea 55 feet below. In July 1964, when the lava resumed its flow, it went rushing over the new sea cliffs, plummeting like a fall of molten gold into the water below.

Perhaps for all observers of Surtsey the most exciting geologic formation was that of the cliffs. (For the cliffs held the lure of life, the possibility that living things might gain a precarious grasp on the island that had risen from the sea.)

◀ *Lava cliffs formed in July 1964.* ▶

8 THE SIMMERING SOUP

When the rime [frost] and the blowing of the warmth met so that it thawed and dripped, there was a quickening of these flowing drops due to the power of the source of heat.

After the gale ate away at the island and created the cliffs it might have seemed that Kolga, Hraesvelg, and Ymir had triumphed over the little upstart named Surtsey. But out of this destruction rose the possibility for life. Their gnawing and lashing at the thin lava edges created a potential habitat for bird life. In fact, birds had come to Surtsey before the the cliffs, when the island was just a couple of weeks old, but only for the briefest visits. It was not a hospitable place.

Sea gulls would alight during the short lulls between explosions; some people speculated that the gulls enjoyed the warmth on their feet during the cold winter. Guillemots came, but not exactly by choice. After the winter fishing season had begun, some of these birds were caught in oil patches left by fishing vessels and could neither fly nor float on the water, so they came to the lonely new island to await death. Other birds came, however, to settle down and nest. A pair of ravens—as well as several pairs of kittiwakes—found the newly formed cliffs where, only six months before, the lava had spilled into the sea.

But could life be sustained? Could new life find its way to the little island and start up?

When Surtsey erupted, releasing gases and tephra into the water, a soup began to simmer. Earth scientists often like to call this kind of soup the *primordial soup*, or the first soup. The tephra and gases contained inorganic substances such as salts, water, acids, and gases such as hydrogen chloride and ammonia. Under the right conditions the inorganic compounds can link up, or synthesize, to produce organic compounds, the essential building blocks for life.

The one ingredient that must be present for a synthesis of organic compounds to happen is energy. The energy can be heat, electricity, or radiation. One alone might do the job. All three were present at Surtsey.

The ocean water was swirling with inorganic molecules—particles from gases, salts, and acids—found in the sea and in the tephra and lava as well. The ocean had been brought to a boil. In fact, the scientists realized the sea

▲ *Bird prints attest to the earliest arrivals on the new land.*

▲ *A geologist and the author leave the scientists' hut in June 1991.*

around Surtsey was truly a cradle of life, perhaps very similar to that first cradle from which life on earth had evolved 4.5 billion years ago.

This region captivated the imaginations of scientists around the world. They would watch and they would wait to see what happened. One thing they had already begun to observe was that existing forms of life were quickly finding a new perch on the island, which had appeared like a strange and desolate moon in the wind-scoured sea.

Surtsey was declared a sanctuary. A Surtsey Society was formed to control who could come to Surtsey and how research on the island would proceed. The Surtsey Society built a small hut in which scientists who came to observe could stay. There were strict rules for those scientists. Pockets and cuffs had to be emptied and clean before arriving on the island to avoid bringing any soil, seeds, or pollutants. All food had to be stored in the hut and eaten in it, too. Leftovers had to be buried, burned, or carried off the island. Special chemical toilets were provided for the scientists so that no human waste would be left on Surtsey. Most important, people had to watch where they walked, to avoid trampling any little shoot or sprout that might be grappling for a hold on the island, where there was no soil, only rock. Since its eruption in 1963 fewer than one hundred people have visited the sanctuary of the island of Surtsey.

But scientists did come. Offshore, fishing boats unloaded scientists into small rubber dinghies that bounced like corks over the tumultuous surf breaking on the black sand beach.

◀ *Scientists observe the action during the violent first year of Surtsey's life.*

▲ *Scientists examine rock formations.* ▼

Often the boats capsized just before landing, dumping scientists and equipment to be washed ashore sodden but happy to be on the newest place on earth. The scientists collected samples of rock and volcanic gases, dissolved ashes in water, and found amino acids—important building blocks for organic compounds. They even scooped up hot lava from craters to analyze it and see what wonderful ingredients might start life simmering in the soup.

All the basic compounds—those building blocks for life—were present in the gases, lava, ash, cinders, and seawater. And the energy was there, too--from the sun, from the heat of the boiling volcano, and from the electricity of the charged vapor clouds that had been sent up with the tephra eruptions scoring the sky with lightning. But Surtsey was of course not identical to that very first cradle of life. One major difference was that Surtsey was not entirely alone as earth had been when it came into existence 4.5 billion years ago. Surtsey arose from a sea that was part of the crust of the planet earth. Earth is no longer desolate. There has been life on earth for 3 billion of the planet's 4.5 billion years of existence. In this new cradle of life there were already neighbors, ready to drop in.

And they did. The birds arrived early on, and in Surtsey's first spring a seal swam around the island and came back for summer visits, as if using it as a resting place. Microorganisms were blown in or crawled from the sea. Whether any would eventually be permanent settlers—whether they would be migrants or real colonizers— was the next big question.

A geologist collects rock samples. ▶

9 COLONIZATION

The earth will shoot up out of the sea and will then be green and fair. Crops will grow unsown.

Although Surtsey stands off by itself several miles from the nearest of the Westman Islands, it is surrounded by paths of water and air, wind and currents, that swirl things near it. It is also on the routes of migratory birds on their flights between Iceland and Europe. And, because Surtsey is the southernmost outpost of Iceland, it is the first stop for birds flying north from Europe in the spring.

Birds are great transporters of other life. Their droppings can supply organic energy. On their feet they bring seeds. They are carriers of small organisms from which new life might start, and even in death their carcasses left to rot on the beach can supply organic materials needed for life.

The champions of the seed-carrying birds over the ocean barrier were the snow buntings from southern Europe that came to visit Surtsey. Botanists captured ninety birds and examined their feet. On thirteen pairs were small shreds from many plant parts, including seeds, tissues and spores of molds, various mosses, diatoms, and other higher plants. Some seeds were found in the droppings of birds or mixed in with the grit in the gizzards of those that had died. From a total of ninety-seven birds that were eventually studied, eighty-seven different seeds were found. And these seeds came from as near as Iceland and as far away as the British Isles and Europe. There were seeds of sedge and of rosemary; there were the seeds of rushes and crowberry. From dissecting one dead bird's gizzard, geologists identified the source of the grit and were able to determine from which of the British Isles many of the seeds came. The grit itself in birds' gizzards could supply needed minerals to the island environment.

Certain plants and animals would most likely never come to Surtsey.

▲ *The fulmar, an ocean traveler*

▼ *A feather caught in lava*

A lost fishing buoy is evidence that ▶
the sea is not a barrier to anything
that floats.

The ocean is a formidable barrier. Many plants need land animals to disperse their seeds. But seeds that are carried by birds, or seeds that drift or sail, have a free ride. Seeds of vascular plants (plants with conductive systems) are often fitted out with feathery plumes for wind dispersal, and it was thus that the groundsel and nuts of cotton grass and others came. Whereas some seeds of vascular plants floated in free and unattached, others came clinging to pieces of driftwood, fishermen's nets, buoys or floats, even plain old trash.

The encapsulated eggs of the skate fish, known as mermaid's purses, were a favorite seed carrier for certain species of plants. The seeds were caught in a firm grip. The shredded outer surface of the purses were as good as burrs for catching seeds. To survive sea travel and salt-water immersion a seed had to be, first and foremost, buoyant. It could not get soggy and sink or rot, or it would never reach Surtsey. And all of these seeds of vascular plants did have another lucky thing in common. They were not entirely dependent on soil. They could derive some of their nutrients from the air.

▲ A mat of seaweed drifts ashore.

Then spoke Gylfi: "How did generations grow from him and how did it come about that others came into being?"

"We call them frost giants. And it is said that when Ymir slept, he sweated. Then there grew under his left arm a male and a female, and one of his legs begot a son with the other, and descendants came from them."

Biologist Sturla Fredricksson found seeds from lyme grass and sea sandwort on Surtsey within months after the eruption. He took the seeds back to his laboratory and indeed they had survived their rough passages either by drifting on a mermaid's purse or on the bottom of a bird's feet. The seeds did sprout in his laboratory. But would they sprout on a beach of lava pebbles and smashed basaltic sand, of shattered black glass? For that is essentially what volcanic sand is. June 3, 1965, was a landmark day in Surtsey's brief history. A single plant of sea rocket was found quivering in the wind of the black beach. This was the first living plant to have taken root on the island. A few weeks later, twenty additional seedlings of this same plant were found to be sprouting. But would they in turn multiply and produce more seeds? That was the next step. Would the pioneer plants become permanent colonists? This island of black cliffs and beaches had a very short season for things to take root and grow. It would take a long time to green, to fill with life.

◄ *A sea rocket, the first vascular plant to flower on Surtsey*

▲ *Mats of sea sandwort* ▼

In 1967 and 1968 sea sandwort and lyme grass began to take hold and colonize. These two plants were among the most successful of those early pioneer species because both were able to germinate. Their ability to cling to the tiniest pieces of substances made them particularly well suited for growing on the black sand. Indeed, as the two species flourished they helped form sand mats that eventually became dunes.

By 1968, however, the sea rocket was established enough to blossom, and it became the first flowering plant on Surtsey. Fifteen of twenty-one plants flowered, and six had mature pods with seeds inside. This meant that the sea rocket was the first of all the plant colonizers that truly had a future. For with the seeds it would multiply, and new generations of sea rockets could be counted on in this habitat. In 1969 a new kind of grass, called *scurvy grass*, was discovered growing on the island. That same year, one of the sea sandworts developed flower buds, promising another generation.

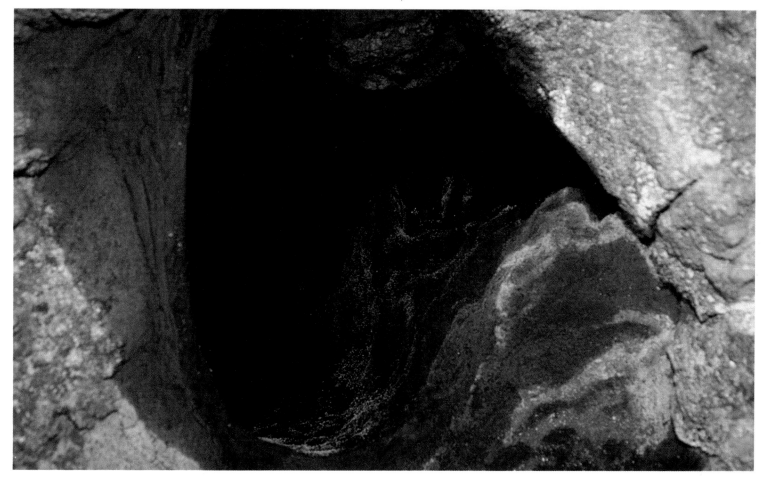

▲ *Moss grows in a crater's vent.*

Other plant colonizers began to produce flowers as well. The sea sandwort, with its waxy green leaves, bloomed with thousands of tiny white flowers. Rafts of pale blue flowers floated from the stems of lungwort. The colonies grew in small, lowspreading clusters, and eventually pale magic carpets of blossoms hovered over the black sand beach and the lava plains. And with the flowers came the island's first butterflies, blown perhaps from the mainland or caught in thermal updrafts. They drank the nectar of the tiny blossoms that clung to the black lava sand.

▲ *Algae at the high-tide line*

After these first pioneers the mosses, algaes, and lichens came to Surtsey. When the ocean surged the microscopic life was washed up against the rocks and sprayed onto the boulders with the foam of the sea. Many of these algae, called *flagellates*, have thin threads or whips—a perfect organ for traveling. Although they might land on the beach they could easily become airborne and be carried to other places on the island by wind or dust particles.

Algae and mosses do not have seeds. Instead they have spores by which they are capable of reproducing. The spores of many of these microscopic plants, or microfauna, that came to Surtsey were very light and could be blown far, often right up to the top of the craters, where they would land and begin to grow on the edges of the still-steaming vents, or fumaroles. They flourished in these warm, moist spots where just beneath the surface the temperatures were well above the boiling point. The rims of the fumaroles became soft with moss, and the big crater, too, was lined with spongy patches of green.

These pioneer plants and microfauna had succeeded in finding a niche in this harsh land so that they could cling, settle, colonize, and eventually reproduce.

◀ Sea sandwort spreads across a cinder field.

Many seabirds, such as the fulmars, guillemots, and puffins, spend nearly nine-tenths of their lives at sea and need only to settle down for brief periods of time. Surtsey, free from predators, was an attractive spot for them because the waters were so rich with fish. In the summer, birds from the south—from Europe and the British Isles—would stop on their way north. In the autumn the migration would reverse. Migrants from the north, as far away as Siberia and the Arctic Circle, would visit. The seagulls were among the very first of the birds to visit, then the fulmars and the kittiwakes, then black-backed gulls and snow buntings. Shortly after the formation of the cliffs the first pair of ravens arrived and became frequent visitors. In 1967 golden plovers arrived, as did several species of geese. In 1968 several ducks as well as a whooper swan arrived. Soon more than sixty different species of migratory birds were making short stops on the island.

The birds would come, alight on the still-warm rocks, fish, eat, excrete. Their droppings became a secondary source of energy for the island, leaving seeds and organic material as well as minerals that would be important to future soil formation. In the beginning Surtsey was not a comfortable place to stay for even brief periods of time. The creeping lava from the crater always threatened to permanently entrap the birds, and the gases from vents swirled through the air. But that first spring kittiwakes and redwings began to rest on the tephra bluffs and the black vertical cliffs just carved out by the April gales.

A fulmar nests on the rocks. ▶

These lava cliffs sculpted by the undercutting of the sea formed a perfect habitat for the birds. In them the birds eventually would build their nests in a lee from wind and weather, away from the heat and the gases of the crater.

These cliff-dwelling birds, which included puffins and a variety of gulls, were the first of the winged pioneers to settle. And in 1970 the first warm-blooded creatures were born—two black guillemots and one fulmar. By the following year there were sixteen more nests.

◀ *Lava cliffs provide a roost for gulls and other seabirds.* ▶

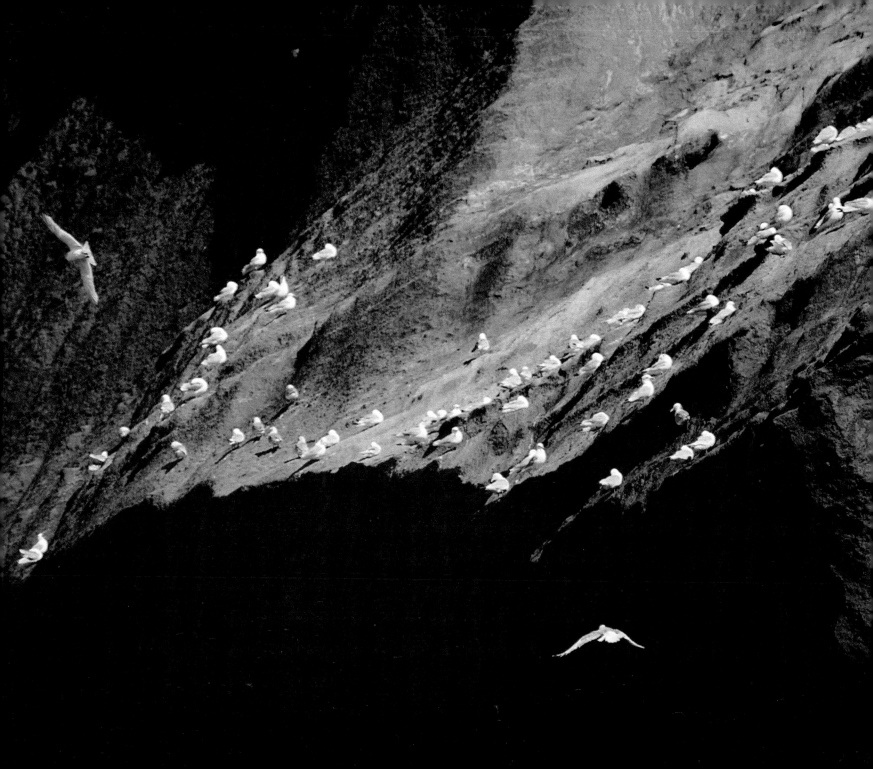

11 THE ENDLESS CYCLE

It was at the beginning of time, when nothing was; sand was not, nor sea, nor cool waves. Earth did not exist, nor heaven on high. The mighty gap was, but [there was] no growth....

The island cooled. The lava boulders once as big as cars were battered by the beating surf and they eroded. The bits were sucked out to sea and swirled back in again to form a sandy black spit of a beach.

The small green star of a seedling sprouted in the black sand. Moss crept slowly across the ropy lava plains, molding itself over the rim rocks like a thin green coverlet to invade the crater. The beach seedling held on, grasping at grains of sand. More sand collected in between the small leaves and shallow roots. The small green star clung to what it could and was clung to in return. The seedling became a spreading plant, a mat of waxy leaves grasping for more sand, holding the beach in its small grip against the sea.

Above the beach the cliffs began to form. The birds came.

Like escaping tendrils from a fire god's hair, wisps of blue vapors still curl out from the craters' vents, a reminder of the event deep in the earth where creation began in destruction.

The island is young, the story is old. The battles are old, too, and there are no clear winners. Aegir, god of the ocean, will never cease. Iord, goddess of the earth, has risen from the fires of Surtur clothed in mosses and blossoms and crowned by a thousand high-flying birds. Kolga of the waves still bashes against the shores, and Hraesvelg, from whose wings the wind comes, still scours and sweeps the cliffs and hills. The forces of nature that brought life will eventually bring an end to Surtsey. The lonely island will become steeper and smaller until one day millions and millions of years from now it will be just a single rock, bashed by the sea. And then there will be nothing—not sand or maybe even sea or cool waves—but perhaps deep within the earth one morning the serpent will twitch.

INDEX